{ *Earlier Poems* }

{ *Earlier Poems* }

FRANZ WRIGHT

Alfred A. Knopf   New York   2007

THIS IS A BORZOI BOOK
PUBLISHED BY ALFRED A. KNOPF

Copyright © 2007 by Franz Wright

All rights reserved. Published in the United States by Alfred A. Knopf,
a division of Random House, Inc., New York, and in Canada by
Random House of Canada, Limited, Toronto.

www.aaknopf.com

Knopf, Borzoi Books, and the colophon are registered trademarks of
Random House, Inc.

The poems in this collection originally appeared in the following:
The One Whose Eyes Open When You Close Your Eyes (Pym-Randall
Press, 1982); *Entry in an Unknown Hand* (Carnegie Mellon
University Press, 1989); *The Night World & The Word Night*
(Carnegie Mellon University Press, 1993); and *Rorschach Test*
(Carnegie Mellon University Press, 1995).

Library of Congress Cataloging-in-Publication Data
Wright, Franz, [date]
Earlier poems / Franz Wright—1st ed.
p. cm.
ISBN: 978-0-307-26566-1
I. Title.
PS3573.R5327EI5 2007
811'.54—dc22   2006048796

Manufactured in the United States of America
First Edition

Pain passes for sunlight at some depths.

—BILL KNOTT

CONTENTS

The One Whose Eyes Open When You Close Your Eyes
{ 1982 }

Entry in an Unknown Hand
{ 1989 }

I

II

The Night World & the Word Night
{ *1993* }

Rorschach Test
{ 1995 }

The One
Whose Eyes Open
When You Close
Your Eyes

{ 1982 }

In the Reading Room

Since I last looked up
from my book,
another appeared in the room
seated at the long table across from me
under the window,
bathed in gray light.

I don't think he has come
to reflect on the lyrics of Verlaine.

The one who with tremendous effort lifts his head
and stares straight at me, and sees nothing;
the one who suddenly gets to his feet
as though his name had been announced.

So far so good, no one has noticed.

Below the readers' faces,
set now in the impenetrable
cast of people sleeping,
pages go on turning
in the silence, so much snow
falling into a grave.

The one with head bent, eyelids closed,
looking at his hands.

Asking for My Younger Brother

I never did find you.
I later heard how you'd wandered the streets
for weeks, washing dishes before you got fired;
taking occasional meals at the Salvation Army
with the other diagnosed. How on one particular night
you won four hundred dollars at cards:
how some men followed you and beat you up,
leaving you unconscious in an alley
where you were wakened by police
and arrested for vagrancy, for being tired
of getting beaten up at home.
I'd dreamed you were dead,
and started to cry.
I couldn't exactly phone Dad.
I bought a pint of bourbon
and asked for you all afternoon in a blizzard.
In Hell
Dante had words with the dead,
although
they had no bodies
and he could not touch them, nor they him.
A man behind the ticket counter
in the Greyhound terminal
pointed to one of the empty seats, where
someone who looked like me sometimes sat down
among the people waiting to depart.
I don't know why I write this.
With it comes the irrepressible desire
to write nothing, to remember nothing;
there is even the desire

to walk out in some field and bury it
along with all my other so-called
poems, which help no one—
where each word will blur
into earth finally,
where the mind that voiced them
and the hand that took them down will.
So what. I left
the bus fare back
to Sacramento with this man,
and asked him
to give it to you.

Reno, Nevada

My Brother Takes a Hammer to the Mirror

{ in memory of Thomas James }

One in the morning: my brother
appears at the back door.
It opens.
Lights are on.
No one is home. The murdered
eyes look in
the bathroom mirror:
It was raining when they buried me;
I traveled, I fell ill.
I can't recall shooting myself
in the head.
Have I said it
before?
It was raining.
He switches the lights off.
All windows are dark
on the block where he stands now,
the stars blazing on
the closed lips
pronouncing these words.
Have I said it before: night
arrives sowing
the mirrors in black rooms with the stars.
Have I said it before?
I estrange.
Light is someone.
Father?

Nocturne

I am the black moon, the blank page, the field
where they dug up
the blindfolded skull.
Think of the roots'
thin fingers
drawn so slowly, slowly
as the growth of hair through
utter darkness
to drink—
that is me.
I am the shade trees growing near graves cast,
the cellar door you have to open
like a huge book,
the bird in the ditch, its beak
slightly parted.
Sober, irreproachably dressed
in a black suit
or with long-unwashed clothes,
the damaged nails,
I come, the representative
of my own nonexistence.
I arrive with my eyes
of the five-year-old child
in a wheelchair, the light
from two stars
dead for a thousand years;

I arrive
with my voice
of the telephone ringing
in an empty phone booth
on Main Street, after midnight
in the rain.

Trespassing on Highway 58: For Two Voices

Horses stand asleep
White shadows cast in at their feet

         It's here that I saw you last fall

Lost in thought huge heads

         For one second

Turn as I pass between stalls
These vast barns house also
The owl and the moth

         My nostrils dilated in shock

The needling mosquito
Galloping rats

         Here I saw you

The drinker comes here
Furtive sighs
Float down from lofts

         Propped up with your back
         To a wall

A single rope hangs
From a beam

Your legs
Partly covered in straw

The spokes of the moon roll across the broad floorboards

A light wind stirred
In the six-feet-tall corn

Your forgotten face follows me back down the road

Dream of Snow: Los Angeles

Toward the end of November
I dreamed that it snowed here

I dreamed that I rose from
the couch
where I had been napping
for weeks
with the lights on

I went to the window

*

As a child
in Minneapolis
I was warned at school
not to eat the snow

As a child
I was drilled
to get my ass up
and my head down
under the desk
where it would be safe
when the glass shattered

*

It says in the newspaper
airports are snowbound
all over the country

A girl in Nebraska is found
in a field
frozen to death in her nightgown
It will be 80 degrees

*

And I
will close my eyes now
and lean back in this chair
and watch the snow
blowing in from the north
over the freeways
over the emptied suburbs
over the gray waves
over the graves of the skyline
over the university
over the Mercedes-filled parking lots
       of the pale physicists

far from you

Arriving in the City

In the loose-fitting hospital gown,
holding a juglike container of blood
like a lantern,
the vein of a clear plastic tube running out of it
up one baggy sleeve,

disheveled and pale, you approached
down the aisle: on the night Greyhound
somewhere between New York City and Cleveland,
I abruptly woke up
with the distinct impression I'd screamed,

the one seated next to me still
fast asleep—I am walking
alone down Third Avenue now—those around me
all still fast asleep.

I find the address—it is on one
of those unlighted, unfrequented side streets
that are like passages
marked in a book
for undiscernible reasons.

The light is on.

I look up in the dark
faintly luminous blue hall of sky

between the walls
of locked warehouses.
Incontrovertibly,
the light is on.

I look up in the moon,
bathing the bones of my face in the cold
of that gray immaterial city
inhabited by eyeless millions, gazing
interminably at the world.

From René Char

To quiet you the poet
Places to his lips
A finger
Whose nail is torn off

*

Often I speak
Only to you
So the earth
Will forget me

*

The peace of dusk
Moves over each stone
Dropping
The anchor of grief

*

With complete sobriety I remain
The mother
Of distant cradles

*

Lightning and blood
I learned
Are one

*

I
Who never walk
But swim and soar
Inside you

*

My future life
Is your face when you sleep

Waking on the Mountain Facing Mount Konocti

If I looked long enough at my hand,
in time
I might picture fine hairlike roots
twining around its fingers. If
I stared long enough,
I could see to the bones—
or with a cold incandescence the bones would start shining.
But I have looked up,
my face ten years older
since I first spent the night here,
and nothing has changed:
over the forehead of Mount Konocti
the last stars are already fading, forgotten.
The hawks' wings catch light, miles above, from the edge
of this world's personal star
minutes before
it reaches my eyelids, which I want closed now
in the chilly wind
that comes as the moon sets.
There is still time.
There is time, and I can still open them
if I wish.

The Earth Will Come Back from the Dead

Down empty roads gray with rain;
through branches
of new leaves then still
more light than leaf;
from turning alone, unperceived, with its sleeping, the wind
the transfiguring wind
in their leaves . . .
from turning, slowly
turning, turning
green
when everyone is gone.

Seeing Alone

Seeing alone
was a door
I walked through
into a higher
and more affectionate
world, dim trees I come upon walking here
                              presenceless
rustling invisibly
rustling

Blood

My blood sits upright in a chair
its only thought, breath.

Though I walk around vacant,
inconsolable,
somebody's still breathing in me.

Mute, deaf, and blind
yes—but someone
is still breathing
in me: the blood

which rustles and sleeps.
The suicide in me
(the murderer).
The dreamer, the unborn.

But when I cut myself
I have to say:
This is my blood shed
for no one in particular.

If I get a nosebleed
I lie down on the cot, lie
there still, suspended
between ceiling and floor

as though the bleeding
had nothing to do with me,

as though I'd been in an accident
but died one second before the collision.

In a hospital room
I have to turn my face
from the bright needle;
I see it, nevertheless,

and I see the blood,

and I see the test tube
in which my nurse carries it
obliviously, like a candle
in a sleepwalker's hand.

Old Bottle Found in the Cellar of an Abandoned Farmhouse

It is still more light
than glass.

*

Though it leans halfway
into the invisible
it has a seam,

like a dress;
it sings
when you blow into its lips.

*

Since it is so empty and clear
it fills up the imagination,
makes me want to bring some well water
in a sieve
after setting fire to the barn
with a magnifying glass in the moon.

Knife

Holding a knife, or imagining it holds a knife, my blood goes to sleep in my fist. If I stare into it long enough, inevitably the moment when I no longer recognize it arrives. This is the moment when the blood unknowingly offers itself to be slaughtered; when cuts can occur like a slip of the tongue; when a little blood could billow in a glass of water and impart to it the disappearing taste of my own life.

Mosquitoes

Playing your trumpets
thin as a needle
in my ear,
standing on my finger

or on the back of my neck
like the best arguments
against pity I know.
You insignificant vampires

who sip my life
through a straw;
you drops of blood
with wings;

carriers
of insomnia
I search for
with a lit match.

I had a job once
driving around in a truck
to look for your eggs.
They can be found

in ditches, near
train tracks, outside
of a barn
in an upright piano filled with rainwater.

It is impossible to kill
all of you,
invisible in the uncut grass
at the edges of the cemetery:

when the dogs go down there it
looks like they've gotten into birds.

Trakl

It is November 1914. I am not very old
yet. Now I almost feel you
place the needle in your arm, dreaming
of the lightvessel in Mary's right wrist,

the wheatfields, the blond cemeteries,
the wind shepherding the dead leaves.
Now I am you walking among trees.
I have walked a long way from my army. I am dead.

I have already slept through the twentieth century,
I've slept through my clothes, through my body,
and nothing remains. I am a blind man who's
sitting with photographic absence in a park

in Vienna, which at twilight is utterly silent
and vacant as only a city I have never
visited can be. Now I am in a small bed,
I can hear myself breathing. I haven't learned to talk.

The Sniper

. . . stopping to light a cigarette
in a crowded street
it suddenly happens,
I'm able to feel

the crosshairs
of a high-powered rifle
randomly focused
on my forehead or chest.

Oblivious to the lit match
in my fingers, I raise
the other hand
to my face

and instantly see myself
through the sights
of the imagined weapon
equipped with a silencer.

It's then I begin to envision
my own thoughts: a black rainbow—,
a hearse filled with water
and driven by men wearing diving suits,

goggles, oxygen tanks. The deceased
allowed to float aimlessly
inside this womblike compartment,

inside this immense tear
lit by the candle
a mourner holds
in her thin rubber hand.

Far from people right around me
I strike another match,

something like a man waiting
in front of a firing squad.
Something like a man waiting
for his photograph to be taken,

in his fingers the seed
of a tree
from which he'll be hanged
in another life.

The Wedding

The photograph's crowded with the dim figures of dimmingly remembered people. People without childhoods. Children dressed in stiff clothes as in grave clothes, for appearance's sake. Trees. It is one of my mother's weddings. There I am, eight years old, already wearing that resignedly griefstricken expression of someone whose life is behind him. In the crowd, my mother and I are still not separated, but it is startling clear that we are now both citizens of another past and that nothing is going to diminish our sense of foreignness in this one. The photograph fades ineluctably; two thousand miles from here my mother's hair turns gray as she combs it . . . Now she looks out at me through years. She sees how I long to torture her white dress. And I turn my face from that awful forgiveness.

The Visit

Almost always, it's just getting dark
when you come back, when you arrive
on this street;
dark
and perhaps just beginning to rain,

as it is, lightly, now.

Lightning
along the perimeter of the black cornfields past N. Professor,
and out back from the nursing home,
where they're putting people
to sleep.

Almost always, it's just getting dark
when I realize you are gone;
when you come here
and lie down beside me, without any clothes on
and without a body.

Drinking Back

From where I am
I can hear the rain on the telephone
and voices of nuns singing
in a green church in Brugge three years ago.

I can still see the hill,
the limestone fragment of an angel,
its mouth which has healed with
the illegible names in the cemetery,

the braillelike names—
the names of children, lovers, and the rest.
The names of people
buried with their watches running.

They are not sleeping, don't lie.

But it's true that once
every year of their death
it is spring.

Initial

To be able to say it: rose, oak, the stars.
And not to be blind!
Just to be here
for one day, only
to breathe and know when you lie down
you will keep on breathing;
to cast a reflection—,
oh, to have hands
even if they are a little damaged,
even if the fingers
leave no prints.

The Wish

I'm tired of listening to these
conflicting whispers
before sleep;
I'm tired of this
huge, misshapen body.
I need another: and what could be prettier
than the wolf spider's, with its small
hood of gray fur.
I'm told it can see in the dark;
I'm told how its children
spill from a transparent sack
it secretes, like a tear.
I'm told about its solitude,
ferocious and nocturnal.
I want to speak with this being.
I want it
to weave me a bridge.

Hand

Striking the table it seems to impose
silence on all metaphysics.
Yet touching the word *sun* in braille
or switching on a lamp, the hand
is clearly the mind's glove,
its sister, its ghostly machine.
You'd hardly call what I feel pity
as I watch it
light this match.
Yet it is the hand of the child
and the corpse in me—
the sleeper's hand, buried apart
in its small grave of unconsciousness;
the hand that's been placed in handcuffs by police;
the hand I used to touch you, once;
the cool hand on my forehead.

The Solitude

You're thinking of the pilot
in his glass cockpit
40,000 feet above the street
you live on
unseen
except for the white line
traced halfway across the darkening sky
all at once it dawns on you
the telephone is ringing
for the first time in weeks
and with equal suddenness
it ceases
as your hand goes to lift the receiver
in the next room
so that when you return to your window
the sky has grown empty the first star

Brugge

{ *for C.P.* }

I have had a strange thought: I see a young woman wearing a bridal dress stretched out asleep on her back in some grass. In an immense field. The sky darkening in another century . . . The sleeper's right hand floats an inch or so above the earth, the string of a kite—too high to be seen—tied around her wrist. There is no one else in sight. I stand looking on at what seems to be a great distance; yet the slightest movements of her lashes, the most insignificant alteration in her breathing, are as clear to me as they would be to somebody kneeling beside her and peering into her troubled, unrecognizable face. I don't approach. I am in no position to touch the alone. I move in and out of their fragile worlds erratically and by complete accident . . . I make one more attempt to place her; but now it's like trying to detect the motion of the minute hand, or watch yourself grow old in a mirror . . . Churchbells. The moon a mile off.

Morning

A girl comes out
of the barn, holding
a lantern
like a bucket of milk

or like a lantern.
Her shadow's there.
They pump a bucket of water
and loosen their blouses,

they lead the mare out
from the field
their thin legs
blending with the wheat.

Crack a green kernel
in your teeth. Mist
in the fields,
along the clay road

the mare's footsteps
fill up with milk.

The Road

I see the one walking this road
I see the one whose coat is thin whose shoes need mending
who is cold it's a very cold day
for stopping beside this dead cornfield
and basking one's face in those gray Rorschach clouds
I see the one whose lips say nothing
I see through his eyes I see the buried radiance in things
the one who isn't there

Those Who Come Back

{ for B. W. }

You are one of those
who came back miraculously
whole. And yet
if someone shakes your hand,
if he welcomes you
into his home, without knowing it
he also welcomes in those who did not:
those who came back with hooks
protruding from their sleeves,
who came back in wheelchairs
and boxes.
They fill the house,
those who came back
with empty pant legs
or black glasses; those who
came back with no voice; those
who come back in the night
to ask you their name.

The Old

Their fingernails and hair continue to grow.
The bandaged eggs of their skulls
are frequently combed by the attendants
and friends no one has mentioned are dead.

A few of them wander around in the hallway,
waiting to be led off to the bathroom.
And these move as if underwater, as if
they were children in big people's shoes,

exploring each thing in their own rooms
for the first time:
mirror, glasses, a vial of pills
with a name typed microscopically on it,

impossible to make out.

Their memories tear
beside places recently stitched.

When I get up in the morning I'm like them
for four or five minutes: I'm anyone
frightened, hungry, somnambulistic, alone.

Wind rustles the black trees once.

Then I grow young.

Brussels, 1971

Some night
I will find myself walking
the sunlit halls of the school for the blind
I used to go past
on my way to the train
on my way to you gliding by one vacant classroom
after another all at once I will stop
inside the doorway
of one where a child
in white shirt and black tie sits
alone at a desk
fingertips pressed to the page
of an immense book
where leaves' shadows stir

and when I wake up
I will not remember
your face won't appear in my mind
and I will lie there a long time
hearing things
the pines outside a car
grinding its engine
a block away
the voice of a crow
this world's chilling star-rise
and I will open my eyes
and get it over with

St. Paul's Greek Orthodox Church, Minneapolis, 1960

There are times I can still
sense the congregation
all around me, whispering
to the one who raised the dead;
the one whose own
pulse had ceased, and yet returned
from the tomb.

His face above
in the high
enormously bright golden dome
of the ceiling:
the Face
so different
from the human

face of Jesus clenched
with agony,
or the beautiful Lord
of Hieronymus Bosch
gently bearing his cross through
the sneering crush.
Each Sunday morning

my speechless lost mother
brought me among them there;
they were mostly old people
on canes, and some I remember
were blind: all of them gone
by now, to their Father's mansion
under the grass.

Poem with No Speaker

Are you looking
for me? Ask that crow

rowing
across the green wheat.

See those minute air bubbles
rising to the surface

at the still creek's edge—
talk to the crawdad.

Inquire
of the skinny mosquito

on your wall
stinging its shadow,

this lock
of moon

lifting
the hair on your neck.

When the hearts in the cocoon
start to beat,

and the spider begins
its hidden task,

and the seed sends its initial
pale hairlike root to drink,

you'll have to get down on all fours

to learn my new address:
you'll have to place your skull

beside this silence
no one hears.

Last Poem

When was it
you first began to pack?
The earth was already, without your awareness,
the earth without you. Because you left
your battered clothes behind. You left
no address. You simply left,
that's all. And when the first star occurred
to the sky—

60 years later, it is still
dusk: it is what happens
when you return,
unseeable, comatose, your empty sleeve
raised above black waters where
the stars' reflections shine
before the stars appear.

The Brother

I'm speaking, of course, on the mirror, the shadow, the other. I'm addressing myself to the dreamer of the body: the one whose eyes open, at night, when you close your eyes. The one who leaves your fingerprints on things you touched tomorrow; whose glove is your hand, whose voice is your muteness, whose sight is your . . . So: inside the darkest room of the darkest house on the darkest avenue in the darkest city, a man is reading a story to his blind identical twin. A man is shaving his blind identical twin. A man is straightening the tie of his blind identical twin. A man is feeding his blind identical twin soup with a large spoon. Now he's helping him on with his coat, they're about to take a little air. As they reach the corner they'll stop, the man will take care to cast a glance left and right before going on; while the brother stands perfectly still, erect, head bowed beneath a black sky in rapt attention to the remote trill of a bird hidden in one of the nearby trees which line this particular street, empty of traffic. All the windows unlit, as you know. No one on earth is awake.

Autumn on West Lorain Street

Go to the window: the dead
leaves stream, soundlessly,
into W. Lorain Street,
frightening with no humans.
It is that time of your day
before Dr. Pierce's young wife
appears below,
tapping her cane
and leading her young
daughter by the hand. Two swans
glide across the lake's black
glass. The marble clouds glide
overhead, their huge reflections
glide across the water, and their shadow
darkens your address.

View from an Institution

Thirty miles or so south of L.A.
stand two hangars, two gigantic tombs
on the plain between
the freeway and the mountains,
remote black swarms of army helicopters every hour
departing and arriving: I still
feel too sick even to think
we lived in their presence
for nearly a year. Oh yes, I remember
it. And when I can't sleep
I think of huge observatories parting soundlessly
or those two domelike structures
we passed once on the coast highway,
the nuclear reactor eerily lit and crane-manipulated all
            night long.
And when I'm by myself,
this is my demented song:
Welcome to the university—
it seems you're the only one registered this fall.
You'll notice our nocturnal sprinkling system.
You'll notice the library's books are all blank on the inside.

To Her

It was still dark out still snowing
You were still here still asleep

When the leaves came out
Their shadows came out too

I can't remember the summer
I can't remember your voice

But it is still dark out still snowing
You are still here

In Memory: 1980

The Journey

9 o'clock. The bells come floating in
from town a mile or so off,
the sky is growing dim now:
not far from my fingers
your photograph is developing
a new expression somehow, more hidden, august.
Why is it disturbing to look at the blind
eyes in a picture;
and how did it happen
that I came to live in a room
with somebody who's not there?
Once, I had to get to
the part of the city
where I knew you were living then,
600 miles away—
and now I will have to relive this,
and hear my footsteps in empty side streets again
and again, the distant, electrical
rustling of late afternoon
foreshadowing rain

as I make my way down your block,
as I ring the door of your apartment.
I find out you live by the East River: I walk there
and sit down on a bench. It's getting cold. I wait
and know nothing, feel nothing, see nothing
but this black river flowing to the sea,
the pale hand on my leg.
A small ship appears with all its lights out.
Now I can remember something
like it from my childhood: a large house
gliding slowly through town on a platform
a foot off the ground
in the summer dusk, the stillness before trains. Sleep
casts its clear and healing shadow over me,
because I have never been this by myself yet
and still have a long way to go.

1973

Home

By twilight, by bat light
I enter the hill where
          it blocks the still luminous sky,
a wake of crickets'
stillness opening
before my feet.

I take the grass road
which winds upward through oaks
          the sun never penetrates;
the creek bed
where nothing is flowing now
but a light breeze.

In back of my shoulders
Orion will rise
by the time I reach the top—
by the time I come to the barbed wire,
where the horses stand quietly breathing in the cold air.
I am that cold, I am not there.

Walnut Creek, California

I Did Not Notice

I did not notice
it had grown dark as I sat there.

Needless to say,
speech no longer came
to your lips even soundlessly now.

You had been out for some time

when, in one slow unwilled motion,
your arm began to rise from the bed,

fingers spread, in a gesture resembling
the one you used to interrupt me,
that we might not miss
a particular passage of music.

Lower East Side Dawn

So flow on my unfathomed river
Shrouded in black music

—IVAN GOLL

I have already considered
the three philosophical problems
worthy of prolonged reflection: Why
are we here?
Is there anything to eat?
Where are our dead friends?

Now it is time
to get dressed.

Behind the wall
I lie facing, the old woman
suffering from gradual disintegration of the spine
and half asphyxiated with
the stench of her own urine
begins another day.
I can hear her now

asking in the little
laughing children from upstairs,
who like to torment her by banging the door,
so she can slit their throats.

And not far from here—not that
far—the long grave

of the river
flows on.

So flow on
my unfathomed horror

black and cold
as space.

As it gets dark tonight
and the two or three stars start to appear
between the bridges and
it can grow no colder,

when the lights come on in the tombs of the skyline,
when the drugged patient hovers a foot above his body,

only tied to this world at the wrist
by the IV needle, futile
hourglass of tears—

I will never again hold your poor
emaciated hand.

I will never again see your
listening face.

The first white crocuses
suddenly appeared
back in Ohio,
one day before
I heard you were gone.

Are you
still here? And if not,
and if not

flow on my black music, flow on
my wind in the hospital hallway—
flow on, flow on
my beginning,
my last address.

March 1980

After

Where I am going now
I don't yet know:
I have, it appears, no destination, no plan.
In fact no particular longing to go
on anymore, at the moment, the cold
weightless fingers encircling my neck
to make me recite, one more time,
the great reasons for being alive.

Permanent address: unknown.
In the first place, we are not convinced
I exist at all. And if I have
a job

it is to be that hour
when the birds who sing all night long wake
and cease one by one,
and the last stars blaze and go out.

It is to be the beam of morning in the room,

the traveler at your front door;
or, if you wake in the night,
the one who is not
at the door.

The one who can see, from far off,
what you hiddenly go through.

The hammer's shadow in the shadow of a hand.

No one,
and the father of no one.

Entry in an
Unknown Hand

{ *1989* }

I

Untitled

Will I always be eleven,
lonely in this house,
reading books
that are too hard for me,
in the long fatherless hours.
The terrible hours of the window,
the rain-light
on the page,
awaiting the letter,
the phone call,
still your strange elderly child.

Winter: Twilight & Dawn

Buson said the winter rain
shows what is before our eyes
as though it were long ago.
I have been thinking about it for days,

and now I see.
And as I write the hills are turning green.
It does that here. The hills turn slowly
green in the interminable rain of late November,

as though time had begun
running backward
into a cold and unheard-of summer.
We are so far from you.

We are as far from you as stars, as those white
herons standing on the shore,
growing more distinct
as night comes—

What a black road this is.
Orion nailed there

upside down, and banking right
into a cloud and descending

behind Mount Konocti.

(The week that marks the beginning
of my life marks
the beginning
of his death

the hour

Rooms

Rooms I (I will not say
worked in) once heard in. Words
my mouth heard
then—be
with me. Rooms,
you open onto one
another: still house
this life, be in me
when I leave

The Crawdad
{ *for Dzvinia* }

The crawdad absorbed in minute excavations;
trees leaning over the water, the breathing
everywhere. And watching alone
a door I have walked through
into a higher
and more affectionate world—,
my face looking back at me, under the water
moss glowing faintly on stone.
We will not sleep, we will be changed.

Joseph Come Back as the Dusk
(1950–1982)

The house is cold. It's raining,
getting dark. That's Joseph

for you: it's that time
of the day again.

We had been drinking, oddly enough.
He left.

I thought, A walk—
It's lovely to walk.

His book and glasses on the kitchen table.

Quandary

{ for Keith Hollaman }

All day I slept
and woke and slept

again, the square
of winter sky lighting

the room,
which had grown

octaves
grayer.

What to do, if the words disappear as you write—
what to do

if they remain,
and you disappear.

To the Hawk

In the unshaded hill
where you kill
every day I have climbed
for a glimpse of you; below me
all the earth turned
golden
in the searing wind, the
very wind golden, its abrupt blast
at a bend in the road
as I approach the summit, shining
wind, where you live
waiting to visit
its own Christless invisible blue and quite terminal instant
on some ex-jackrabbit, plummeting
upward, or floating
suspended
past sight-nimbus: close eyes
beholding themselves in the sun.

Audience

The street deserted. Nobody,
only you and one last
dirt-colored robin,
clenching its branch
against the wind. It seems
you have arrived
late, the city unfamiliar,
the address lost.
And you made such a serious effort—
pondered the obstacles deeply,
tried to be your own critic.
Yet no one came to listen.
Maybe they came, and then left.
After you traveled so far,
just to be there.
It was a failure, that is what they will say.

Alcohol

You do look a little ill.

But we can do something about that, now.

Can't we.

The fact is you're a shocking wreck.

Do you hear me.

You aren't all alone.

And you could use some help today, packing in the
dark, boarding buses north, putting the seat back and
grinning with terror flowing over your legs through
your fingers and hair . . .

I was always waiting, always here.

Know anyone else who can say that?

My advice to you is think of her for what she is: one
more name cut in the scar of your tongue.

What was it you said, "To rather be harmed than
harm is not abject."

Please.

Can we be leaving now.

We like bus trips, remember. Together

we could watch these winter fields slip past, and
never care again,

think of it.

I don't have to be anywhere.

At the End of the Untraveled Road

Under Konocti
the long eucalyptus-lined
road in the moon,
wind of November,
the now hawkless
hills
      turning green—
it was always here, not yet remembered.

Whatever it is

I was seeking, with my tactless despair:
it has already happened.
And I'm on my way now,
the pages too heavy to turn,
the first morning lights coming on
over the lake. How happy I am!
There's no hope for me.

II

Vermont Cemetery

Drowsy with the rain
and late October sun, remember,
we stopped to read the names.
A mile across the valley

a little cloud of sheep
disappeared over a hill,
a little crowd of sleep—
time to take a pill

and wake up,
and drive through the night.
Once I spoke your name,
but you slept on and on.

Morning Arrives

Morning arrives
unannounced
by limousine: the tall
emaciated chairman

of sleeplessness in person
steps out on the sidewalk
and donning black glasses, ascends
the stairs to your building

guided by a German shepherd.
After a couple faint knocks
at the door, he slowly opens
the book of blank pages

pointing out
with a pale manicured finger
particular clauses,
proof of your guilt.

North Country Entries

Do you still know these early leaves, trans-
lucent, shining, spreading on their branches
like green flames?

And the hair-raising stars flowing over the
ridge late at night.

No one home in the house by itself on the
pine-hidden road,

or the 4-story barn up the road, leaning on
its hill.

The two horses who've opened the gate to their
field, old, wandering around on the lawn.

The sky becoming ominous.

Which is more awful, a sentient or endlessly
presenceless sky?

Birthday

I make my way down the back stairs
in the dark. I know
it sounds crude to admit it,
but I like to piss in the backyard.

You can be alone for a minute
and look up at the stars,
and when you return
everyone is there.

You get drunker, and listen to records.
Everyone agrees.
The dead singers have the best voices.
At four o'clock in the morning

the dead singers have the best voices.
And I can hear them now,
as I climb the stairs
in the dark I know.

The Note
{ *for C.D.* }

Summer is summer remembered;

a light on upstairs at the condemned orphanage,

an afternoon storm coming on.

She heard a gun go off and one hair turned gray.

Somehow I will still know you.

The Talk

Aged a lot during our talk
(you were gone).
Left and wandered the streets for some hours—
melodramatic, I know—
poor, crucified by my teeth.

And yet, how we talked
for a while.
All those things we had wanted to say for so long,
yes—I sat happily nodding
my head in agreement,
but you were gone.
In the end it gets discouraging.

I had let myself in;
I'd sat down in your chair.
I could just see you reading late
in the soft lamplight—
looking at a page,

listening to its voice:

yellow light shed in circles, in stillness,
all about your hair.

Ill Lit

Leaves stir overhead;
I write what I'm given to write.

The extension cord to the black house.

Word from Home

Then I went out among the dead
a pint of whiskey in my head
and lay on a mound
covered with snow,
and closing my eyes to the blowing snow

looked into his face.

Smiling and wincing,
reading his shoes,
holding out a ruined hand;
wishing for a way to disappear—
all the poor formalities of the mad.

As if I had met him years later,
an accident—something is wrong with his face.
Thinner, perhaps, the eyes cruel
with pain, my own
reflection in a knife.

The look of love gives the face beauty.

We look at him
as if he were a stain.

We look at him.

Entry in an Unknown Hand

And still nothing happens. I am not arrested.
By some inexplicable oversight

nobody jeers when I walk down the street.

I have been allowed to go on living in this
room. I am not asked to explain my presence
anywhere.

What posthypnotic suggestions were made; and
are any left unexecuted?

Why am I so distressed at the thought of taking
certain jobs?

They are absolutely shameless at the bank—
you'd think my name meant nothing to them. Non-
chalantly they hand me the sum I've requested,

but I know them. It's like this everywhere—

they think they are going to surprise me: I,
who do nothing but wait.

Once I answered the phone, and the caller hung up—
very clever.

They think that they can scare me.

I am always scared.

And how much courage it requires to get up in the morning and dress yourself. Nobody congratulates you!

At no point in the day may I fall to my knees and refuse to go on, it's not done.

I go on

dodging cars that jump the curb to crush my hip,

accompanied by abrupt bursts of black-and-white laughter and applause,

past a million unlighted windows, peered out at by the retired and their aged attack dogs—

toward my place,

the one at the end of the counter,

the scalpel on the napkin.

Duration

On the sill
the blown-out candle

burning
in the past.

Frozen clouds
passing over

the border
north. Listen

to the end,
listen with me.

III

No Longer or Not Yet

From a phrase by Hermann Broch

In the gray temples of business

In the famine of the ant-bewitched seed

Wolves attacking people in the half-deserted suburbs

And kings dead with their hands crossed on their genitals
a thousand years from now

In sunlight shining on your vacant place at the table

In the sneer and the kick in the face world without end

In my crouched shadow loping beside me

In the imbecilic prose of my thoughts

In the voice of the one fingerprinted blindfolded and shot

World of dead parents unconsciously aped without end

In the hand above the rainbow horses of the Pêche-Merle cave
        walls

We interrupt this program to bring you the announcement that
        enemy ICBMs will begin to arrive in
        ten minutes

In the strangeness which corridors and stairwells have for children

Death of the weekday

In their parties alone in a sip from an empty cup

In the little grass toad beating in your palm

The spider spinning in the dust the barren worm

The death of tears

In the gashed vivid colors of gas station restrooms at
        three in the morning

(And we thank Thee for destroying the destroyers of the
        world)

In the unaccompanied boy on the Greyhound the old woman
        with a balloon

World no longer or not yet

In the moon which goes dragging the ocean and turning
        its chalky steppes away

Unsummonable world

In the white stars in the black sky shining in the past

The black words in the white page uttered long ago

Death of tears

In the storm of wordless voices the hand abruptly
        shocked into dictation

(Envelop me clothe me in blackness book closed)

In early March crocuses pushing deafly through soil

While you quietly turn between dreams like a page

The morning light standing in the room like someone who
        has returned after long absence
        younger

World no longer or not yet

IV

Look into Its Eyes

The leaved wind,

the leaved wind
in the mirror

and windows, perceived
by the one-week-old.

Forever, we weren't here—

Biography

The light was getting bad;
he wished the rain would stop.

He'd try again tomorrow—
anyway, he had to walk.

Brain-sick. Wet pavement. Green neon.

The light was getting awful—
had to walk the ghost.

He'd try again, he wished.

He'd try again.

The Day

My mother picks me up at school.
Strange. I leave the others playing,
walk to where she's parked—
and why are we driving so slowly?

You have to turn right here, she whispers.
When we get there the whole house is silent.
Why's that? Does this mean
I can watch *The Three Stooges*?

Evidently. She's driving away now,
and he's not in his basement typing:
he isn't there at all, I've checked.
This must be my lucky day.

Night Writing

The sound of someone crying in the next apartment.

In an unfamiliar city, where I find myself once
more,

unprepared for this specific situation

or any situation whatsoever, now—

frozen in the chair,

my body one big ear.

A big ear crawling up a wall.

In the room where I quietly rave and gesticulate—
and no one must hear me!—
alone until sleep:

my life a bombed site turning green again.

The sound of someone crying

There

{ *for Thomas Frank* }

Let it start to rain,
the streets are empty now.
Over the roof hear the leaves
coldly conversing in whispers;
a page turns in the book
left open on the table.
The streets are empty, now
it can begin.

Like you
I wasn't present
at the burial. This morning

I have walked out
for the first time
and wander here
among the blind
flock of names
standing still
in the grass—

(the one on your stone
will remain
listed in telephone books
for a long time, I guess, light
from a disappeared star . . .)
—just to locate the place,
to come closer, without knowing where you are
or if you know I am there.

Poem

{ *for Frank Bidart* }

Per each dweller
one grass blade, one leaf
one apartment
one shadow
one rat

By itself, defending a lost position,

the poem
         writing the poet—

Anvil of solitude

So diminish the city's population
by one, and go
add your tear to the sea

Heart that wonderfully lasted
                      until
I learned how to write
what it so longed to say

Nothing of the kind.

A Day Comes

A day comes
when it has always been winter,
will always be winter.
Witnesses said the crowd fled
through the park, chased by policemen on horseback
past the Tomb of the Unknown
Celebrity as the guard
was being changed,
but they are gone.
The witnesses are gone.
A day comes
when the planet stops turning.
It is February here,
late afternoon.
It will always be late afternoon,
neither dark nor light out.
But we cannot be bothered,
because we are asleep;
the door is locked.
Now and then somebody comes and knocks
and goes away again
back down the hall,
back down the stairs.
But we cannot be bothered,
because we are asleep
and listening,
listening.
Do you hear the wind?
We have always been asleep,
will always be asleep—

turning over
like pages on fire.
Where were we?
We were listening.
No, I don't hear it either.
The wind, the marching
boots, the burning
names.

Three Discarded Fragments

From the notebooks of Rilke

Who can say, when I go to a window,
that someone near death doesn't
turn his eyes in my direction
and stare and, dying, feed on me.
That in this very building the forsaken
face isn't lifted, that needs me now

*

That smile, for a long time
I couldn't describe it—
the velvet depression
left by a jewel . . .

*

A child's soul like a leaf light still shines through

The Street

On it lives one bird
who commences singing, for some reason best
known to itself, at precisely 4 a.m.

Each day I listen for it in the night.

I too have a song to say alone,

but can't begin. On it, surrounded by blocks of
black warehouses,

is located this room. I say this room, but no
one knows

how many rooms I have. So many rooms how will I
light

This isn't working out, is it

Here's what really occurred, in my own words

I murdered my father—and if he comes back, I'll kill him again—but
first I persuaded him to abandon my mother. Now you know. It was
me all along. Then I got bored, held a knife to her throat, and forced her
to marry the sadist who tortured my brother for ten years.

I feel bad about it, but what can I do.

I mean we're talking about a genetic predisposition here.

I *am* taking my medication. And things have gotten a lot better.

And if I ever finish writing this, I'm going to tear that bird's head off and eat it.

My Work

The way I work is strange.

For one thing, you would never call it work.

Although I'm good at that.

Work is not the term.

It destroys me, I adore it—

I'll look at it someday and noticing its utility
still fails to surpass that of a lyre locked up in
a glass case tuned an octave above human hearing,

I'll take an ax to it.

I'll stop speaking to it.

I'll sit alone in some shithole and inject it
until the jewels roll out of my eyes.

I don't know what all I'll do,

snow of
            unlit afternoon . . .

mute and agreed-to
descent

Coordinates

Waking up at an improbable hour
in the small gray-lit Boston apartment
where I can never bring myself
to believe I actually live;
going off in the winter morning to teach
certain there's been a mistake,
knowing as I enter the classroom
the students will look in my face
with unanimous amusement
and lack of recognition,
that before I can utter a word
someone in a suit will appear
and ask me to come with him.

*

This won't hurt at all.
It does?
Well we haven't been taking good care of them
have we. Difficulty explaining to some
the concept of financial terror—
specifically, that if you're afraid to buy food
if you can help it you are not going to spend
$1,500 on a tooth;
difficulty of explaining anything
with your mouth clamped open.
Under anesthesia

I walk along a sunflower field I know of

*

It was still day
when I boarded the train.

The tunnel

then the Charles,
and soft blue lights of traffic in the rain.

*

Everyone in his right mind is asleep.
A black car glides past,
in its wake (the

speed blossoming coldly

through fingers and spine)
a prolonged Coltrane scream

and a shiver of beauty open the night

Waiting Up

I can remember you
mentioning once
how you'd wait until your mother was preoccupied
or gone, to dress
the doll all in white
for its little funeral—
how all the while it stared into your eyes
with its cold unbeckonable eyes,
and seemed to smile.
Why this
I couldn't say. And then again,
why not? It's easy
to remember anything.
I'll walk now, maybe.
The clouds' stature slumberously building
and blooming on the horizon,
identityless, huge
gesticulations from the trees,
a bird's voice
hidden back in the leaves,
the remote barely audible wake
from the roar of an airliner's engines
fill the dim morning.
Maybe your presence
will startle me now;

maybe I'll rise from
this chair.
Maybe the room will be empty.

The room will be empty,
and you will not come.

Guests

Smell of winter pine trees in the air;
around me night, the wind, Marie, the stars.
Last night I dreamed I stood here,
this very spot—why I've come—
lights on in a house across the valley
where there is no house.
Stood here as I lay beside you
and looked so fondly at those lights
they might have been our home, and why not?
Everyone you see
lives somewhere.
How is this done?

Winter Entries

Love no one, work, and don't let the pack know you're
wounded.

Stupid, disappointed strategies.

Hazel wind of dusk, I have lived so much.

Friendless eeriness of the new street—

The poem does not come, but its place is kept set.

Going North in Winter

The sound of pines in the wind.
And to think you're the only person on earth
isn't hard, at the end
of the long journey nowhere.
Yet in the end I have come to
love this room and be the one
looking out on snowfields, blank
scores of wire fence in the deepening
snow, the wind through them a passage
of remembered music, bare
unbeckoning branches
with never a ghost
of a deciduous rustling,
the stilled river
with the sheet over its face—
going north in winter.
And it's all right
to glance out the window:
the fear will grow less
or more intense, but
it will always be there. Unseen
it's a palpable force,
isn't it. Like electricity
which can be employed,

as has been pointed out,
to kill you in a chair
or light your room.
But I'm through with that now.
I reach over and switch on the dark.
It's all right to pronounce a few words
when you're by yourself, and feel a little joy.

The Night World &
the Word Night

{ 1993 }

Illegibility

Hawk in golden space

Thick-leaved, darkly
beckoning trees
bigger than the house

Sunlit apparitional
peaks of a thunderhead
fading
to the east

Page
from conception to death mask

The stranger who approaches on the
    street and says, You
    don't remember me

Occurrence

I've gotten everyone who hurt me.

In a blackout a man loads his shotgun
again.

Outside the genuine star-spangled twilight
of North Dakota
unfurls, twinkling and barking.

Then *he* becomes a ghost.
Big windblown rags of bitching crows
resettle
in the trees out back.

Pawtucket Postcards

Neon sign missing a letter

Firearm with an obliterated serial number

There's always death
But getting there—
you can't just say the word

Rhode Island Artificial Limb Co.

Lights of the abandoned
households reflected
in the little river through the leaves

The posthistoric clouds

Provincetown Postcards

Wolf stars

Owl's head moth

Icon-yellow twilight

Sound of leaves & sea the silent sun

Will all have had ample experience when the last loneliness
comes

Harbor bells in the blizzard

Loneliness

Say you wake
in the night
abruptly alone
in the midst of addressing
vast stadiums . . .

Or at an intersection windows
shattered your forehead
leaning on the horn
a crowd materializing a light
snow beginning

Like the taste of alcohol to children

No

That with which there is nothing to compare

Say you have no friends, or
say you have to go to sleep

To see your friends

There

It's not so bad
the stitches itch
where they removed
your rage
is all

Where they removed
those thoughts

And no one
misses *them*

After several weeks
everyone learns
how to tie his own shoe

You get a little doll that looks like you

Words

I don't know where they come from.
I can summon them
(sometimes I can)
into my mind,
into my fingers,
I don't know why. Or I'll suddenly hear them
walking, sometimes
waking—
they don't often come when I need them.
When I need them most terribly,
never.

Forgotten in an Old Notebook

Outside the leaves are quiet
as their shade. Hidden
inside them a bird is waiting
for it to get dark
to try its goodnight voice.
I have just looked in the mirror,
and come and sat down at the table.
What happens to our faces?

Gone

I dreamed you came and sat beside me
on the bed

It was something that you had
to tell me

I dreamed you came and sat beside me

Like a drowning at a baptism

Like an embittered shopper returning

The sad misspelled obscenities on men's room walls

Snow on dark water . . . Something

After Rimbaud

While the child's forehead, eaten with red torments,
Appeals to the white swarm of indistinct hallucinations,
Appear at his bedside two big charming sisters
With slender fingers and silver nails.

They seat the boy beside a wide-open
Window, where tangled flowers float in the blue air;
Where their long and terrible fingers can walk
Seductively through his heavy damp hair.

He hears their timid breathing's chant, the viscid
Fragrance of the honey of vegetables and roses,
Now and then interrupted by a startled hiss: saliva
Or the desire for kisses sucked back from the lips.

He hears their black eyelashes flicker in the perfumed
Silences; within his drunken sleepiness
The stained nails of their sweet, electrified fingers
Crackle with the deaths of tiny lice.

Now the wine of laziness rises inside him:
A sigh into a harmonica, delirium.
He feels a longing to weep which rises and fades
Again and again to the rhythm of their caresses.

Certain Tall Buildings

I know a little
about it: I know
if you contemplate suicide
long enough, it
begins to contemplate you—
oh, it has plans for you.
It calls to your attention

the windows of certain tall
buildings, wooded snowfields
in your memory where you might cunningly vanish
to remotely, undiscoverably
sleep. Remember your mother
hanging the cat
in front of you when you were four?

Why not that? That
should fix her. Or deep drugs
glibly prescribed by psychiatrists weary
as you of your failure to change
into someone else—
you'll show them
change.

These thoughts, occurring once too often,
are no longer your own. No,

they think you.
The thing is not to entertain them
in the first place, dear
life, friend.
Don't leave me here without you.

August Insomnia

He slowly replaced the receiver
like somebody who had just used it.

He slowly replaced the receiver
like somebody who had just used it
to strike himself
hard,
several times,
on the skull.

Midnight, blue leaves swarming against the glass.

The pregnant child alone on her front doorstep,

the starving moon.

He slowly replaced the receiver.

Jamais Vu

Whether I grow old, betray my dreams, become a ghost

or die in flames
like Gram,
like Frank,
like Thomas James—

I think for a while I'll come back
as a guest to a childhood room
where the sun is the sun once again
and the wind in the trees is the wind
in the trees, and the summer afternoon
the endless summer afternoon
of books,
that only happiness.

I won't have written this.

Smell of leaves before rain, green

light that shines not
on, but from the
earth—

for me, too,

a hunger darkened the world,
and a fierce joy made it blaze
into unrecognizable beauty.

Night Said

I lay on my back in the yard,
my face among the stars.
Night said, Don't go inside.
There's murder in the house,
but that is far away;
don't answer when they call.

They used to call and call,
but it was so dark in the yard.
And I had gone so far away—
guided by the stars
I could set out from the burning house
and watch them sink inside.

I tried to stay inside,
thinking perhaps you would call,
cause silence in the shrieking house:
if I were in the yard
the voice behind the stars
might never find the way;

plus you can't be out there always.
You are compelled to come inside
at some point, leave the stars
abruptly when the strange man calls
your name into the long black yard,
obey the catastrophic house.

I knew I had a real house,
with a real father, a ways—

some states—beyond that yard.
I was a happy child, inside.
Until my name was called
I lay on my back filling with stars,

I raised my hand amid the stars.
Tumultuous leaves hid the bright nightmare house.
Happy and evil for a moment, I called
drop H-bomb here—a little ways
from me, a bird spoke once. Inside
someone flung open the door to my yard,

but called my name into an empty yard.
By now the house was only one more star—
unwithstandable inside, but just a jewel-light far away.

The World

Mood-altering cloud of late autumn

Gray deserted street

Place settings for one—dear visible things . . .

The insane are right, but they're still the insane.

While there is time let me a little belong.

The Forties

And in the desert cold men invented the star

Untitled

I basked in you;
I loved you, helplessly, with a boundless tongue-tied love.
And death doesn't prevent me from loving you.
Besides,
in my opinion you aren't dead.
(I know dead people, and you are not dead.)

The Lovers

Who knows but before their closed eyes
both faces change
in slow reverse

recapitulation
of the faces
each has never seen again:

fetally then
full-blown, in a moment
taking on the different

features of their secret
genealogies
of lovers,

until each has the face
that first troubled the other's
and both sleep with a stranger in their arms.

Untitled

This was the first time I knelt
and with my lips, frightened, kissed
the lit inwardly pink petaled lips.

It was like touching a bird's exposed heart
with your tongue.

Summer dawn flowing into the room parting the
curtains—the lamp dimming—breeze

rendered visible. Lightning,
                                and then soft applause
from the leaves . . .

Almost children, we lay asleep in love listening to the
rain.

We didn't ask to be born.

Say My Name

I'd be entombed
inside a period

in the closed book
in the huge dark

of St. Paul's
where we used to meet,

                    wafted

downaisle toward
banked sunlight-colored candles.

I'd be in your mouth,
in that huger dark:

body that stands for the soul.

Word that means you are loved.

For Martha

You are the bright yellow spider who hides in the apricot
leaves, watching me work.

You are the redwood shade pouring down around me in
blond columns, and you are the air

coolly and goldenly
scented

as the certainty of sleep
when I lie down weary

and at peace, and as the certainty that I will rise again

sane and refreshed— . . .

And my bright yellow spider hiding in the apricot leaves.

For a Friend Who Disappeared

Just one more time. Only one—
the small rose of blood blooming in the syringe—
one to compel haunted speech to the lips,
sure. Some immense seconds pass. Dusk's
prow slowly glides right up Avenue B;
the young Schumann's two personalities
continue discussing each other
in the diary. Your eyes
move to the warning
on a pack of cigarettes—
good thing you're not pregnant!
Still no speech, but no pain either:
no New York,
nothing,
sweet.
You happen to know that you're home.
And how simple it was, and how smart
to come back: in the moon
on its oak branch
the owl slowly opens
its eyes like a just-severed head
that hears its name called out,
and spreads its wings
and disappears;

and the moth leaves the print
of its lips on the glass, lights
on the lamp's still-warm bulb,
the napper's forehead,
his hand, where it rests
down the chair arm,
fingers
slowly opening.

Untitled

Sicklemoon between thunderheads in the
blue of four in the afternoon

And when the first star occurred to the sky— . . .

Why did one write
such things? Not
to describe them—
they don't need us to describe them.
But to utter them
into existence,

just as they *looked at us*
into existence . . .

To give back to them
the existence perceiving them
bestows on us—

just to say them:

to say and feel said,
feel somehow at home here.

Time to Stop Keeping a Dream Journal

This time I dreamed I was writing a dream down

And later on that gray April morning—an out-of-
the-house experience!—

the cemetery blanketed with robins

I held my shadow's hand (he leadeth me)

Hour when each human reports
to the mirror

Leafprints in the sidewalk
unidentified flowering
lavender shrubs
in an otherwise black-and-white
landscape, I pass
through an evil rainbow

A pair of glasses found in a pile of dead leaves: one
of the stations of my day

(Orders, orders, orders: yes, Your Absence—no, Your
Nonexistence . . .)

And inevitable night again 1 a.m. leaves' sounds the
empty moth still clinging to the screen

Shape of leaf mouth eye—the spider in the iris—

And the great trees rustle the moon staring into the
sockets in the grass

And 2 o'clock streets filled with teenagers in fascist drag

And in five years you see them collecting at bus stops
like dust

And still the hand will sleep in its glass ship— . . .

Lament

I took a long walk
that night in the rain.
It was fine.
Bareheaded, shirt open: in love
nobody gives a shit about the rain.
I suddenly realized that I would hitchhike
the 60 or so miles into Kent—
it was so late
I could make it by dawn,
and see the leaf-light in late April
called your eyes. The evil
we would do
had not yet come. No one but me
knows what you were at that time, with
a loveliness to make men cry
out, haunting beyond beauty.
We had what everyone is dying
for lack of, and let it
finally just slip away.
I will never understand this.
I was at the time a relatively intelligent
person. Only
terrorstricken already
at what my life would be—that what I longed for most
would be exactly what I'd get
at the price, sooner or later, little by little,
of everything else,
every last fucking thing.
Yet that morning exists, it must,
it happened. And the years we had—

those almost endless summer afternoons and nights,
a solitary hawk sleeping on the wind, your
incandescent whiteness emerging from the water
in the moon, or snow
beginning, horizontally, to fall as you fall
asleep with your head on my shoulder while I drive . . .
where are they? They exist, the way the world will
when I'm dead. I won't be there
but another nineteen-year-old idiot will be
and to him I say: Don't do it!
But he will—blinded, spellbound, destroyed
by the search for something
he can never see or touch,
when all the while he holds it in his arms.

Midnight Postscript

{ for my friend Joseph Kahn:
born 1950, drowned 1982 }

Walking the floor after midnight
I leaf through your pharmacopoeia
or a book on stars.

How I love the night.

It should always be
night, and the living with their TVs, vacuum cleaners
and giggling inanities
silenced.

With here and there a window lit a low golden mysterious
light.

I love the night world,
                              the word night.
Book & door. Joseph. Death's leaves— . . .

I'm never going to get this right.

And I can't go on forming
and tasting your name
or biting down in blinding pain
forever—no,

from now on I have entered
                              and live in our unspoken words.

And the space I took up in the world scarlessly closes like water.

The Winter Skyline Late

I walk, neverendingly
walk

hating the sleet

the odd million gray disgraced
looks you will meet on the subways
                                     the streets
everything
that will hurt you today . . .

As I have walked these after-midnight
streets so many
years, unwelcome and alone

stopping a minute at some frozen pay phone

gagged on my pride
                        and moved on

                Moonset, dawn:

Konocti

                Venus-lit
greenish horizon

apples
       shadow-dappled
in the early wind . . .

It might have been, somehow

Not now

Eating fear, shitting fear, convulsed
with tedium and horror
every time I went
                    to touch a pen to paper

Crying
in a downtown porno theater

But in our own eyes we are never lost

Looking at the skyline, late
some see the site of triumphant
far-off celebrations
to which they weren't invited
some see a little light
left on for them
and some
the final abrupt unendurable radiance blooming

Local bar of deceased revelers

Special subway station for distinguished lunatics

Cold stars beyond the Charles,
                        ward of bandaged eyes
that turn and stare in my direction as I pass

Black wind and distant lights
I prayed
that I might disappear

Unfather, unsay me
I asked
irreparably here

But why are we drawn walking at night
to certain unfamiliar
solitary places
   Why
this interest in a stranger's lights
Whose ghosts are we

What happened to our faces

The wind moves slowly, fingers
read my forehead
eyelids
lips

The constant sight
of what might have been
aged them
Their million mute
unnoticed acts of insubordination
and inconsequential
cruelty changed them—

Yellow window
in the blue dawn
lost is lost
and gone is gone but
be there
if I wake again, don't abandon me
defend me.

Clearlake Oaks (I)

Konocti's summit
sunlit
on the other shore . . .

To sleep in the mountains
(when have I
ever slept) blissfully
sown

through an infinite imageless brightness—

inspected and forgotten by a grass-green dragonfly.

Clearlake Oaks (II)

The hawk rises
into the sun;
the lizard goes testing the dust
with its tongue—

stationary
hour, above
the windless
blond and shadow of the hill.

And I am
here to say this,

my mysterious
privilege and joy.

Mercy

I embarrass you, don't I—
whining for change
and making you quicken your pace;
or worse staring as you pass by,

without the tact to disappear and die.

The Drunk

I don't understand any more
than you do. I only know
he stays here
like some huge wounded animal—
open the door and he will gaze at you and
                    linger
Close the door
and he will break it down

The Angel (I)

{ *in memory of Marguerite Young* }

Decay of a tone, decay of the sun

Green eyes unseen among the leaves

The reader's lips
              the dreamer's lids

Moon dissolving under the tongue

            Messenger
from a word a noun
with an imaginary corresponding
entity in space

            The human
face about to come

            Midnight's
world-altering
name

And someone gives birth to a child

And laboring someone
gives death to himself

The objects in the room lit up with pain

The Angel (II)

No one loves them because they are ugly

They are ugly because no one loves them . . .

One of the racists of beauty

I feel three green voices
                        gazing at me—

My very existence
inexpiable—

the gardener at the tomb.

The Angel (III)

—the reality of the imagination

—KEATS

In 4 o'clock in the morning insomnia's
eeriest men's room—dropped in on
while driving alone around
town—after catching a glimpse of
my face in the minutely blood-
spattered mirror, suddenly
into my mind, God knows from where,
comes the vivid thought of
transformations the face undergoes
when it is crying:
its ugliness.
How ugly it is.
When it ought to become beautiful
to whoever looks on—
not just any stranger's, but even the most beloved face
grows ugly! How can this be?
Aren't we most human when crying; and if
we are most human, then
aren't we approaching
(we can only approach)
a condition beyond
what is human? I think
the angels must look something like this,
like somebody weeping—only *there*
this expression is seen as one of great beauty
and a sign
of unsurpassable happiness.
And yet

can one speak of the angel at all?
The angel is a word. This
sound of human breath exists:
thus to the mind rendering visible
a being. And whether this being
occupies a place in space
is irrelevant, of no concern
to the physical being crying alone
and the unsayable solitude
of a grief for which I would like to envision
an unseen companion without
whom—let him be a word,
a sob, a thing imagined—
we are the ones who do not really exist.

Theory

What do I care about
walking erect,

the fingers freed
to clutch large sticks, the hand
to hide behind the back—

bared teeth
slowly learning to form
an expression of welcome and pleasure . . .

Man was born
when an animal wept.

The Door

Going to enter the aged horizontal cellar door

(the threshing leaves, the greenish light
of the approaching storm)

you suddenly notice you're opening the cover of an
enormous book.

One that's twice as big as you are—

but you know all about that:

the groping descent alone in total darkness,

toward—what?

You know what you're looking for, and you forget; and
maybe you have no idea

yet. But you know something is down there, and a
light you need to find,

before you can even begin to search.

Thoughts of a Solitary Farmhouse

And not to feel bad about dying.
Not to take it so personally—

it is only
the force we exert all our lives

to exclude death from our thoughts
which confronts us, when it does arrive,

as the horror of being excluded— . . .
something like that, the Canadian wind

coming in off Lake Erie
rattling the windows, horizontal snow

appearing out of nowhere
across the black highway and fields like billions of white bees.

Before the Storm

The poem seeks not
to depict a place
but to become one—

synonymous
              summer
and loneliness . . .

Mute child-ghost
of yourself
at the screen door

Tidepool: Elk, California

Skirting such thick undulating underwater
hair, the unseen

crevice-haunting eel,
the handlike crab

and moon-dilated anemones,
I remember

hunting the tremendous boulders'
undersides—, how then

armed with these
long knives we pried

the abalone's
unrelenting

nursing
from its stone.

1969

Untitled

I have to sleep to think sometimes—
waking into sleep
where you find a world reversed
where muteness is speech, blindness
sight, deafness music
that haunts you alone, and that place
exists where the poem is not
written; it is the wrong
word; where the need to write
is not.
And the tedious prose of the world vanishes
from its ruined page leaving nothing
but the effortlessness of a window
looking out on precisely what is, i.e.
the unsayable mystery
pronouncing itself;
text one has long sought to translate,
even if poorly, only to read it—
here for some moments
weirdly improved on.
Without wearing out one's knees
or gnashing of teeth
or pulling out of hair
or disappointment, or terror
or life darkened, permanently;

but with a return
to the original
gratitude:
as once at fifteen
for perhaps half an hour—
I remember and await

Elegy: Breece D'J Pancake

We can always be found
seated at a bar
the glass before us
empty, with our halos
of drunk flies—
or standing
in the dark across the street
from the Sacramento
Coroner's. (And my friend
we're all in there
floating along
the ceiling, tethered
to our laughing gas canisters.) We are
old people shopping,
next winter's ghosts,
the prostitute
in her mortician's makeup
strolling York Avenue at 3 a.m.,
the fellow in Atlantic City
furtively pawning a doll.
Quick suture,
lightning,
hush-finger—
cheap eeriness of wind chimes—
summer thunder
from a cloudless sky . . .
The abandoned abandon.
There are no adults.
You're dead,
but look who's talking.

The Spider

For a long time I was attracted
to small things. Spiders
particularly: the spiders
who lived in my house

were simply not to be found
although I had no wish to
harm them. It's true
I might have frightened some

in my sleep, I might have
stepped on one without
seeing it, friendly. I did
see one once

but it ran off
very quickly, like someone
who notices a large
crowd coming forward to stone him.

Something about the thin shadow
of a nail in the wall;
the trees' shadows
moving on the bed

while a being casts
its two inches of vision
from a remote corner of the ceiling
into the room.

Once, at dawn, when I was sick
I went through the house
with my drug-lit eyes,
I stopped by the window

and sat down at the piano
in order to type something
about your childhood:
a sip from an empty cup,

a doll cemetery.
A spider appeared, creeping
toward my fingers
like a little furry hand.

I lie down,
I press the place behind my ear
where the vein is.
Today

I observe the absence
of my brother
sentience: the spider
who lived in my room

with its minute blood.

Bild, 1959

As the bourbon's level
descended in the bottle
his voice would grow
lower and more
indistinct, like a candle flame
under a glass

Sunlight in the basement room

So he reads to me
disappearing
When he is gone

I go over
and secretly taste his drink

Mushroom cloud of sunset

Whispered Ceremony

After Char

Like a kneeling communicant offering his candle

the white scorpion has lifted its lance and touched
the right spot.

Ambush has instructed it in invisible agility.

Swollen currents will ravage this naïve scene.

Narcissus, gold buttons undoing themselves in the
field's heart.

The king of the alders is dying.

Train Notes

Voicing
in itself
was the allowing to appear
of that which the voicing one saw
because it once looked into him . . .

Green desuetude of railroad
tracks, wild
apples, aging limestone
angel's face and
changing
cloud

Green lightning past the last trees, they are pure gaze

I am wandering through the corridors of a deserted
                                  elementary school

I am flying
            over a dark sea

Jolted awake
I meet my own eyes
in the window staring back
from badly executed features

(Like a scar the face speaks for itself)

But irises, iris—a meteor,
chrysalis, a woman's

name, a flower's
unconscious light

Green eyes the altering light alters

Unlit
    until the sun

Damned to language, we come from the sun

From stars and weather flowing in opposite directions
Stars slowly silently flowing
and setting,
beginningless

Rorschach Test

{ *1995* }

Voice

I woke up at four in the afternoon. Rain woke
me. Dark. Mail—a voice said, You'll have
mail,

scaring and gladdening my heart. Enough anyway
to get it to leave the bed, attempt to make coffee,
dress and begin limping downstairs. All

the boxes were empty. Of course. A voice said,
He just hasn't come yet. But I knew: it is four
in the afternoon—the others have already taken

the mail indoors. Hours ago. If this my box
is empty now then it was always empty.

Rain. Darker

now. By the time I had walked, more or less,
back up the stairs, the treacherous voice had
nothing more to say.

Hope. They call it hope—

that obscene cruelty, it never lets up for a
minute.

But not anymore—never again. If the telephone
rings just don't answer it, said the voice. Very
adaptable, the obsequious voice. If the mail does
come put it in the garbage with its fellow trash;

or set it on fire in that big metal can in the alley,
you know, your publisher. Dark. Odd. It was
light when I finally slept, I hear myself saying so
out loud. I suppose I am insane again,

on top of everything else. He talks to himself now,
they'll say. Who. By the time you get back to your
room you won't even exist. A bit mean now. And you
will sit down in the chair with your back to the
window, it observes.

After a little I know for a fact you will open your
notebook and write all this down,

why I don't know. No doubt you will even show it to
somebody, at some point: they'll talk to you, offer advice,

admit admiration for this phrase,

dislike for that. But they don't understand. You don't

care now—how can you. No, I don't care what they say,
what they do to me now. I used to. Terribly. And then you didn't.

And then I didn't.

Infant Sea Turtles

Think of them setting out from their leather beached eggs
to follow the moon to the sea
and into the sea.

The ones who make it. Think of them

hatching, so strange—like some misshapen
birds who haven't yet grown wings.
But no, they are far in advance of that, returning

to the sea that vast tear we came crawling out of.
Led there by what we call the moon:
Eve, or cesarean child.

The moon which left the great scar called the sea
when it tore itself from the earth's side
and flung itself out into space,

lover or child, to escape—but not far enough.

The Comedian

I was mad when I got home
and smelled the alcohol.
I thought he was sleeping, though
the color of the skin, the
breathing and the drool were strange.

Impossible to touch him or get near.
He started, as I guess
I sort of barked at him through tears.
All I asked for was an ambulance
I'm sure, though don't remember phoning. Cops

searched for drugs in my empty film canisters.
Nobody really saw *me*.
The "Final Wish," as he put it
in the almost illegible note that was pinned
to the wall like a crucifix over the head

of the bed of some lonely serious child:
something having to do with cremation
and scattering ashes on the Ohio. And do you know
I laughed. I actually laughed—what does he think this is—
left by myself in the house. It was a scream.

Heaven

There is a heaven.

These sunflowers—those dark, wind-threshed
oaks— . . .

Heaven's all around you,

though getting there is hard:

it is death,
heaven.

But they are only words.

One in the Afternoon

Unemployed, you take a walk.
At an empty intersection
you stop to look both ways as you were taught.
An old delusion coming over you.
The wind blows through the leaves.

Beginning of November

The light is winter light.
You've already felt it
before you can open your eyes,
and now it's too late
to prepare yourself
for this gray originless
sorrow that's filling the room. It's not winter. The light
is. The light is
winter light,
and you're alone.
At last you get up:
and suddenly notice you're holding
your body without the heart
to curse its lonely life, it's suffering
from cold and from the winter
light that fills the room
like fear. And all at once you hug it tight,
the way you might hug
somebody you hate,
if he came to you in tears.

The Meeting

I happened to be in a strange city
drinking.
One of those dives where you enter
and just pull the covers over your head;
where the gentleman sitting five inches away
has lately returned from his mission in space
in the one coeducational toilet stall
existing on the premises,
and will continue to sit there forever, nodding
and peering down into his shot glass
like a man struggling to keep awake over a bombsight;
and the aged transsexual
whore who never got around
to the final operation in his youth
seems to be pursing her lips
in your direction, demurely, down bar.
One of those places with windows
the color of your glasses—
a fact which in no way compels you
to remove them. Nobody cares
about your eyes: they'll go on serving you
as long as you can talk,
as long as you can still pronounce
your drink by name and are tactful
enough not to fall off your stool
or call anyone's attention
to the fetus in the vodka bottle
to the left of the vast Bartender's
telepathic, "Another?"
It was then you walked past,

outside the window, unhindered
by the event's complete impossibility.
This kind of thing's happened to everyone.
No? Never mind, then:
I will describe it.
At whichever ground zero
you've found yourself waiting, waiting,
there is one and only one person
whose sudden dumbfounding appearance
could, if not exactly save you,
afford you some respite
from the slightly green outpatient
you're supposed to be keeping an eye on there
behind the beverages in the mirror, the one
whose job is watching you . . .
Then she walks by.
Though the instant this transpires
you know it's already too late,
she's vanished right back again
into one of those infinite places
where you are not. And it's pointless
to run to the door, tear it open and scream
her name into the freezing wind:
it doesn't stand a chance
of being heard above
the amused roar of the sky's numberless sports fans.
No—you need a strategy.
Needless to say, this calls for a drink or ten.
Now this individual, her special haunts:
there is still a very slight chance
they are all in your mind, that grim city
that's changed somewhat since you've been here
attending your dark little party.
And God only knows what's happened to the one

outside the door, a place
you have never really been to
and one where you never intended
to do a lot of sightseeing.
You are a peaceful man.
But what can you do—time's passing faster,
and your loneliness is ruined anyway.
You down your shot of fear and hit the street.

Late Late Show

Undressing, after working all night,
the last thing I see is the room

in the house next door.
At four in the morning, a dark room

filled with that flickering
blue

so familiar, almost maternal
if you were born

in my generation:
this light

so intimate, reassuring you
that the world is still there

filled with friendly and beautiful people, people
who would like to give you helpful products—

adoring families—
funny Nazis . . .

                    Undressing, the
last thing I will see.

Heroin

And now it's gone
I'll wait
for time to come
and tuck me in

a little white blank
envelope,

and mail me
on this pretty wind-lights

midnight:
I am safe

here in the darkness,
the gloating

vampire
of myself,

waiting for the sudden light
to open, its enormous hand

to sort me from the others
and raise me up

and finding me spotless, devoid
of destination or origin,

transport me
to the painless fire
of permanent, oblivious
invisibility.

Rorschach Test

To tell you the truth I'd have thought it had gone out of use long ago, there is something so nineteenth century about it,

with its absurd reverse Puritanism.

Can withdrawal from reality or interpersonal commitment be gauged by uneasiness at being summoned to a small closed room to discuss ambiguously sexual material with a total stranger?

Alone in the presence of the grave examiner, it soon becomes clear that, short of strangling yourself, you are going to have to find a way of suppressing the snickers of a ten-year-old sex fiend, and feign curiosity about the whole process to mask your indignation at being placed in this situation.

Sure, you see lots of pretty butterflies with the faces of ancient Egyptian queens, and so forth—you see other things, too.

Flying stingray vaginas all over the place, along with a few of their male counterparts transparently camouflaged as who knows what pillars and swords out of the old brain's unconscious.

You keep finding yourself thinking, God damn it, don't tell me that isn't a pussy!

But after long silence come out with, "Oh, this must be Christ trying to prevent a large crowd from stoning a woman to death."

The thing to do is keep a straight face, which is hard. After all, you're *supposed* to be crazy (and are probably proving it).

Maybe a nudge and a chuckle or two wouldn't hurt your case. Yes,

it's some little card game you've gotten yourself into this time, when
your only chance is to lose. Fold, and they have got you by the balls—

just like the ones you neglected to identify.

Reunion

Movement of the hour hand, dilating
of the rose . . .
Once I could write those.
What am I? A skull

biting its fingernails, a no one
with nowhere to be
consulting his watch,
a country music station left on quietly

all night, the motel door left open
to Wheeling's rainy main street, the river
and wind
and every whiskey-breathed

ghost in the family—
left open,
old man,
for you.

Depiction of Childhood

It is the little girl
guiding the minotaur
with her free hand—
that devourer

and all the terror he's accustomed to
effortlessly emanating,
his ability to paralyze
merely by becoming present,

entranced somehow, and transformed
into a bewildered
and who knows, grateful
gentleness . . .

and with the other hand
lifting her lamp.

Night Watering

A big velvet-brown moth
with an eye on each wing, asleep
right in the middle of
the sunflower, its antennae stirring
lightly now and then. We are alone
on this dim barely window-lit street—
stirring, maybe because of the light
breeze or a semiattentiveness
to my presence in its trance,
an inability to decide
if something's really there,
combined with a total indifference
since it has found at last its golden
temple of the myriad gold chambers
and its god. The flower
has virtually tripled in size
since bursting into bloom a week ago, in fact
it's grown so huge it is in danger
of breaking its own neck.
(It reminds me of someone we know.)
I spend about an hour
rummaging around the back porch
for twine and poles and so forth—it's beginning
to get blue out now—and finally
manage to prop up the head
so it will be comfortable.
At this point I am beginning
to appreciate the cool, still night
and it is almost gone. Now the moth
all this time has not budged

from its spot, it will not be disturbed
at its devotions. I stand in my own
fascination and envy, more
difficult to break at this point.
At last I return
to the house from this four o'clock watering,
happy for once
to have something important to tell you
when you wake up, when I
lie watching while the golden
petals of your eyes begin stirring, then
startlingly open
all pupil, meet mine
and cannot decide what I am
or if I'm really there.

Planes

Dream clock—next port of entry— . . .

By diurnal moonlight, by dream clock, by star-blueprint
it approaches

*

Over here they are sharpening
the seeing-eye
knife,
etc.

*

Her hand on my

shoulder
without a name

*

Tempus fuckit

*

Funny, I sometimes feel like a motherless child (trad.)
too, unknown
black voice

*

Friends never met

*

Put in the dark
to hear no lark

*

Heart with a miner's face

*

Poem, my afterlife

Blue underwater statuary

And when the sky gives up its dead . . .

*

Thank you, I've just received yours

Unless all these years
I've been misunderstanding

the verses. In any event

I'll scratch your back,
you knife mine

*

 And when the sky gives up its dead

And the dead rise blind and groping
around for scattered bones, the skulls
they don like helmets
before setting out, bumping into another sadly
as they hoarsely cry
the full name
of some only friend

The Weeping

He *has* considered weeping, only
he can't even bring himself to

take a stab at it. He just can't cry—
it is terrible to cry

when you're by yourself, because
what then?

Nothing is solved,
nobody comes;
even solitary children understand. This
apparent respite, apparent quenching

of the need to be befriended
might (much like love in later years) leave you

lonelier than when you were merely alone?

Untitled

The unanswering cold, like a stepfather
to a silent child

And the light
if that's what it is

The steplight

No—

the light that's always leaving

The Family's Windy Summer Night

The moon on her shoulder
like skin—
brightest and nightest desire.
Her eyes, unknown to him,
wide open. Dark
for dark's sake, he recalls:
the fallacy still
unavoidable.
Child,
the glass of sleep
unasked for and withheld.

The Leaves

I have been sitting here
all of the past
hour very sleepily watching the wind
as it blows through the black leaves
surrounding the house
in absolute silence, the leaves
swarming like huge moths' wings
in a futile but tireless attempt
to come through the windows. I am so tired,
I don't understand it:
I can barely keep my eyelids open,
barely remain sitting upright.
I have been by myself
far too long watching the wind
blow through the black-green leaves.
It has been so long
since anyone has called;
I can't remember the last time
I heard the doorbell ring.
And even if it did,
what difference would it make.
I don't detect the vaguest desire
to get up and answer the door,
to see another face. No,
I could quite easily remain here
like somebody pleasantly lapsing
into deep sleep, a sleep so profound
no phone or alarm clock or doorbell
could ever reach its lightless depths.
I really have to rouse myself, maybe

even call up a friend I have missed;
or go for a walk in my neighborhood's
shady decrepitude (where do they go
when August comes, where
do they all disappear to) . . .
And I fully intend to, I certainly should—
just give me a minute or two,
I am so incredibly weary
and I don't know why. I think
these leaves are wishing me
asleep.
That must be what it is.
I must have left a window open.
I can hear them all at once—
they've gotten in somehow
and now
they are covering my body. My face,
they are covering my face;
and I have passed the point
where I might have lifted a hand
to brush them away,
if I'd wished to.
I am drowning, I think:
I have been drowning
now for a number of years,
and I have had the strangest dream.

Ending

It's one of those evenings
we all know
from somewhere. It might be
the last summery day—
you feel called on to leave what you're doing
and go for a walk by yourself.
Your few vacant streets are the world.
And you might be a six-year-old child
who's finally been allowed
by his elders to enter a game
of hide-and-seek in progress.
It's getting darker fast,
and he's not supposed to be out;
but he gleefully runs off, concealing himself
with his back to a tree
that sways high overhead
among the first couple of stars.
He keeps dead still, barely breathing for pleasure,
long after they have all left.

The Mailman

From the third-floor window
you watch the mailman's slow progress
through the blowing snow.
As he goes from door to door

he might be searching
for a room to rent,
unsure of the address,
which he keeps stopping to check

in the outdated and now
obliterated clipping
he holds, between thickly gloved fingers,
close to his eyes

in a hunched and abruptly
simian posture
that makes you turn away,
quickly switching off the light.

Twelve Camellia Texts

The thought of the camellia unfolds

*

The camellia you placed
in the mirror

One of those that chooses you
nights
when you can't sleep

On the cool floor at your feet
lies one that fell
unnoticed the moment you entered

like a shooting star . . .

               Nights
when you look up
afraid all at once

Anything can happen here

Every star in the sky may be nothing
but light that still reaches your eyes
though each of them died
                    disappeared
as many years ago
as people will live on
the earth

Then who will see
the camellias that are breathing all around you
who will care
              and yet
the hand with which you hold the stem
is still real

                              *

Waxy roselike petal eyelid of a sleep
you need never return from
though your head falls
at last
into a sleep even deeper the double
of your life before you were

                              *

Motionless uninterrupted
by the open window
still

as a candle's flame under a large glass

perfectly vertical
pointing
at the sky

sunrise sky mirrored in the camellias

before it disappears

                              *

Motionless yet growing

Tensed faces of the newly dead
growing young again
before our eyes

at the speed of the hour hand the moon
setting on the hill

*

Leaves evergreen immortal
for a little while

Formal
the unbreathing
the seemingly unbreathing
manifold flower that exists like the earth
before and beyond life
here forever
approximately

Oh live while you are here

*

Flower mysterious commonplace

Let's say of you in particular
why do you exist
when no one would notice if you'd never been
if you'd never breathed
like any human presence
like the world
the universe . . .

Mirror of creation
beauty itself

for no reason
miracle

beauty itself
or a torch that's passed on
both
as Agee noted

its face and sex are one

*

No one has seen the invisible rainbow
arc of your fall

Longhaired star of the peripheral Vision

All we imagine but cannot perceive
or believe in
or instantly forget

Our own life a parenthesis
of light

then abrupt transition
to an unknowing

where dark ascension
and falling
are one and the same

*

You reflect the hidden wildness
waiting in the wings of earth's

statelier weather
The undivulged grieving
of homesick faces

Dark green hair's-breadth vein or
rivers flowing
            returning

to a little spot in Asia 1660

                    *

Evergreen even in shade
nocturnal
bloom at noon

Breathing one another
what garden can contain them

Nagasaki
            the Apple Blossom . . .

Under a glass sky
each one has its own star
all the sun it requires
for the time being

                    *

Apparitional
once you appeared
in the Pacific northwest

No one was scared
the fools

An exotic curiosity perhaps

you had found a place that felt a little like your own
and were promptly placed under a jar
or glass house

At that time people sometimes
just moved on the glass house fell
into decay

Lightning maybe or
slow-motion shattering
silent over time
And to no one's surprise

no one being there at the moment

the resurrection of your white face rose
there in the frost
in your reversed
mirror world like Persephone's
darker twin sister

who dies of spring

Your newly awakened
groped toward the cliffs
salt crystallizing like honey the petal-tongues
tasting the familiar
wind tasting their exile

blindly gazing toward Japan

*

Camellia scent
too subtle for the mind (perhaps
someday when the mind is human)

we've been given your visible
presence
            nobody knows why
We don't even know why
we were given our own

But who would choose smell over vision
As post- or prehumans we are accustomed
to disagreeing over everything
it seems to be our job
there's nothing we do better
                    and any fool can do it
It's like breathing no doubt we would perish
if it were to cease for five minutes

But in your presence could anyone ever
            deny
would anyone dare deny

it's a good thing you are here

Camellia visible as wind
moving the leaves
                moving our hearts

Camellia of the one-starred sea at dawn.

The Blizzard

You sit in the unlit room watching
a storm as it slowly erases the street
and the neighbors: on one side
the mother of four
armed and dangerous grade-school-aged children,
and on the other those night owls, proprietors
of an open-all-night drive-by crack store.
You sit in the darkening room
gazing at the vanishing skyline
in the distance. How long has it been?
The room completely soundless.
Night wind around the house, the ticking
snow against the windows—
for some time you've ceased to hear them
or anything else, only the silence
such constant nearby noises
finally come to. The same
way the music has passed into silence
even as you listened, yet remains
filling the air, your very presence
flickering in a last
awareness of itself.
You are wide awake, your eyes are even open;
yet you only notice this music
which you carefully chose for yourself
long after it's ceased. And you wonder
where you might have gone
during this absence: it seems
to be night here. Yes,
it is night in the room.

But here, too, is a lamp within reach
on a small familiar stool-like table
beside you, beside the large chair
which so closely resembles the one
in which you are sitting. You reach across
to switch on this lamp and are shocked
by the telephone. You sit back and inhale
the black air deep into your lungs,
and listen to it ringing.
Then, for a while, to it not ringing.

Mental Illness

A metaphor
one in which
the body stands
for the soul
who's busy
elsewhere
no doubt floating
facedown
down
a black reverie

Poem in Three Parts

1. The Gratitude

By no longer being

here,
you've made it easier for me to leave the world.

2. The Wound

The wound that never healed but learned to sing.

3. Version of a Song of the Ituri Rain Forest Pygmies

The darkness—where is it?
Surrounding us
all.

If darkness is, darkness is good.

The Face

Is there a single thing in nature
that can approach in mystery
the absolute uniqueness of any human face, first, then
its transformation between childhood and old age—

We are surrounded at every instant
by sights that ought to strike the sane
unbenumbed person tongue-tied, mute
with gratitude and awe. However,

there may be three sane people on earth
at any given time: and if
you got the chance to ask them how they do it,
either they would not understand, or

I think they might just stare at you
with the embarrassment of pity. Maybe smile
the way you do when children suddenly reveal a secret
preoccupation with their origin, careful not to cause them shame,

on the contrary, to evince the great congratulating pleasure
one feels in the presence of a superior talent and intelligence;
or simply as one smiles to greet a friend who's waking up,
to prove no harm awaits him, you've dealt with and banished all harm.

Depiction of a Dream (I)

I think I have murdered a child.
It happened earlier today
while I was taking my nap.
I have to take these naps,
you see, because I never sleep.
And they usually serve well enough
as a means of reminding me
and sometimes revealing
facets, heretofore hidden,
of my terrible character. And yet
such numbing and saddening and
unimpeachable representations of it
are rarely required; the routine betrayal
of somebody who cares about me, the opportunity
to be betrayed and voluptuously wallow
in that, the conviction I'm being pursued
by unknown individuals who wish me harm
or death do the job for the most part. This time
I have murdered a child, I think
he was quite a small child, one of those
who can walk—sort of—and say a few words;
who still emit the faint light
which exists nowhere else, is a bit like
the radiance certain dim stars shed
only when your eyes are turned away
and perceive it peripherally, yet remains,
clever similes notwithstanding,
wholly beyond the power to describe.
It seems to me I'd been entrusted with him,
a little boy belonging
to neighbors I don't know,
and we found ourselves holding hands, walking

along the precarious margin
of some deafeningly traveled freeway;
then for some reason his tiny hand
(you know, one you might crush like an egg
merely by clenching your own slightly) slipped
through my hand and he suddenly
turned left
and stepped into traffic. Immediately
he was grazed by a car moving past
at too great a speed for the driver
even to notice, was spun to the ground
where I rushed to his side with a heart attack
managing to help him to his feet,
the left shoulder shattered, eyes conscious
but blank. We were able to enter unseen
the woods to the right, where I half ran,
gripping far too tightly his right hand, slashed
blind by low branches.
Abruptly, we came to
a lake shining brilliantly
just past a stand of pines.
I don't understand what happens next. Yet
what was I supposed to do? How could I
take him home in this condition?
I grabbed him by the ankles
and with one swing smashed his head
against a big stone. Now
he had no head and I had this small, almost
weightless object to dispose of. I put him
in the water and he vanished. I returned
to the house of his parents, and found them there
preoccupied with many other children,
hoping insanely no one would notice
the absence of mine and rehearsing,

the same way I have all my life,
a plausibly sorrowful lie
about the child that I had lost.
Trying to find my way out of the darkening
forest, the incomprehensible task
accomplished, leaving just one more, one
equally loathsome: surviving,
denying everything, trying
to go on without being killed
again.

Depiction of a Dream (II)

So far I have eluded them.
I don't have the faintest idea what I've done.
I do know it must have been terrible:
at this point every other person on the street
looks as if he could be a plainclothesman;
and whatever they did with the half of the town
they replaced, they were splendidly trained
in mimicking those former citizens' sullen
opinion of my presence,
their indifference to my comings and goings,
to the fact that I exist at all. I'm trying to get home.
A group of men approaches as I cross the park.
One of them is a good friend I remember from school,
one I lost contact with years ago. How wonderful!
I feel happy and safe for the first time
in so many months. We grin and embrace.
He asks about my life. I tell him
I will be teaching again very soon.
I'm afraid it won't be soon, he remarks,
with a sinister failure to alter the warmth in his voice
or the broad smile.
All at once the cuffs are on—
someone's soundlessly come from behind—
freezing through to the bones
of my wrist, like they do,
although he hasn't moved or ceased to gaze into my eyes
with the same protective look of sadness and delight
you develop at encountering some beloved person
long considered dead, or forever lost to you.
There are, incidentally, a couple of gun barrels

touching my head, coldly branding
their zeros in my temples.
The others all stand in a ring
surrounding me.
I start to cry.
I have to feed my cat first!
I have to feed my cat.
What's going to happen to my cat.
I think you had to be there.

New Leaves Bursting into Green Flames

This is why somebody loves
the poem, or attempts to
make up his own verses, in other words
devote his life to something
that's generally held to be
an occupation solely of the dead,
and so impossible. (In terms of livelihood
this is, in fact, correct.)
Those who inhabit the rest of this block,
the greater part of the city, the planet, to them
it is impossible, irrelevant, and again
on account of its clearly nonlucrative
nature, contemptible: but I will tell you
why one sits writing his poem, which is nothing
in the end but the longing to locate
the door to his own happy world
forever locked in his face otherwise;
to therefore see the world in terms of words, and pay
the price for this, in a strange
key. There is no point to it, one passing through this
fire, yet involved's an indomitable thirst
to attempt, without knowing how,
knowing only you're going to fail,
saying back to the earth
a few words which equal
or even rival its beauty,
its loneliness,
its disappointment and wrath.
And for what? My landlord never heard of me

and expects his rent just the same
as he expects it from the junkies,
giggling sophomores and cowering eccentrics
with whom I share this building.
I have gone on with it. I don't know why
except that I've never loved anything else,
its possibility anyway;
and it is the only thing that has never
permanently turned its back on me. And so
I've gone on, in this absurdly ugly place—
I have yet to hear a single note
of that famous still sad music.
I've done it for the sake
of maybe 10 minutes when I was fifteen:
when I—when it suddenly—but why describe it?
No one will understand, no one will care
that today, while waiting for the bus
I looked up from the tedium
of untreatable things
and found them again,
here. The few newborn
leaves more light
than leaf on a branch.
They were back—or I was.
For an instant no time had elapsed:
these leaves were not new,
they were the same ones, and I was not old.
Nothing had changed, they were the same
leaves that blazed before
my eyes all those years ago, mind blazing.
That moment so long ago,
I did not have to say, was this moment.
How could I go to the hospital

for my appointment now,
when I had gotten well?
So I just turned and walked
home. (I call it home.)
Having nowhere else to turn
this is where I generally go.
What difference does it make anymore?
And it was fine. I had not lived
my whole life in vain—
nothing had damaged that instant
those minutes I had lived
for all my life.
And anyone, in the words
of André Breton, who smirks at this
is a pig.

The Lord's Prayer

I have been attempting to pray
the Lord's Prayer for the first time
since I was a child. Only now
the problem is not one
of mystified indifference, on
the contrary. Now
my concentration is eclipsed
by many distractions, though I'm trying to mean it.
One question now is the existence
of the mad. One of the most bothersome
things about the mad:
they are so often right.
Look at Christ. And yet
as they are, after all, insane
most don't possess the social graces,
the finances or tact
that would be required, so
there is virtually no question
of their influencing or getting anywhere near
the circles where the true and the delusional are
               legislated.
I think of Pilate, eyebrows slightly raised
in weary but astonished sarcasm,
responding to the assertion, "I come
to bear witness to the truth." It's horrifying
but I can never read this, that is
P.P.'s reply, "What is truth?"
without having to suppress a strong impulse to agree.
This is the abomination of the secret

envy the sane feel for the mad with their constantly
                menaced
yet suicidal willingness
to say what's true with a clear conscience;
envy of the torturer
who will be going home soon, disgusted
and tired from his day's legal work
to supper and family.
We've grown a good deal more cunning—
compassionate, we call it.
Still, we don't take any chances.
We keep them under control—just think,
when we could so easily kill them
just like in the old days
of family and morality. But it's an easy task,
since they are incapable of taking any action whatsoever
save that of occasionally perceiving
reality. The real one.
We do this for their own good, of course;
they might hurt themselves, you see, especially
                us.
And we have any number of methods
which involve both their concrete surroundings
and the medicinal alteration of their capacity to
think. I mean, look where it got them.
For no one, absolutely no one
harbors the slightest desire
to be reminded of reality.
Things are bad enough as it is.
I myself have served with a believer's heart
on both sides, and I must say
I greatly prefer the company of the nuts, though
I will side with the sane any day.

I will freely admit to being a little confused
by this. It's not so much a matter
of Lowell's off-the-cuff remark, "I am inclined to
                believe
that it is better to be happy and good
than to be a poet."
It isn't that simple. In fact,
it is excruciatingly mysterious.
But perhaps the human race is not
all dressed up in mystery at all, but
in reality is the Void
in pathetically transparent drag, "or something."
"So to speak."

Where You Are

Dawn finds you leafing through old address
books.

You thought you had written to everyone.

Yes, you have. To everyone—some of them

also wrote to you. They wrote back to you. Years
ago, now. You aren't there anymore.

Then what do you want them to say. Nothing has
changed, nothing has happened

to them—the ones who lived, the ones still at
the same address. How would you ever describe
it. And why.

And what could they say. They are safe.

They have a life, why would they want to write.

Untitled

I like to see the individual verses
spread on the otherwise blank sheet of paper
like lines of black cocaine. Unfinished,
unincorporated into something anyone is ever going
        to see:
they are mine, to deny their existence
and share with no one, as I please. They fill me
with joy while they're still unemployed, still about to be
rising up through the trunk-spine and leaf-veins of the brain: before
I shudder, close my eyes and see nothing
but light where there's supposed to be nothing.
Then open them on a new room,
one with a window outside of which
a different world has appeared, one
embodying euphoric intimations of a life-
beckoning beauty, death-beckoning
beauty, what do I care—
I've entered my vacant room as I must, only
this time to find a nude woman who's kneeling
with her slender forearms resting on the sill,
who tosses her hair to one side as the breeze
from the window blows through it, its dark blond
torrent floating, color of a horseman's torch
at dawn, and stares in my direction
over her shoulder, sees no one and almost

smiles before her eyes
return to the window I, too,
continue to gaze out of,
unless I do dare to approach her, letting this page
go totally blank once again and the mere
words all blow away.

Black Box

The great black star-spoked hours
pass slowly
slowly
all morning long . . .

When I look back
from here it seems
all children must sense
some vast inheritance

being withheld

life itself kept
deliberately from them
by their family the strangers

yet they all know the secret
of midnight
and wage a futile war for years
to stay awake
and see it

dawn

a black box of stars
you could conceal
in your fist
if you knew where
they kept it

The combination
undivulged
unknown perhaps
except to those
who do know where it is

The ones who command it is late
go to bed

And you do
for the time being
In fact they are right
it is late now

for them
very late

All the while you are aware
it is early

and getting earlier

One day I was suddenly wakened
I'd finally escaped I don't know where
or how I had managed it

Me

But somehow I was free
I also had the box it was

still under my pillow where else
like a gun

I was abruptly awakened
by eight numbers spoken in turn
by a circle
of eight diamond voices
identical
still vivid in my mind's ear

I reached for it and it was there
beneath my ear
and now

I also possessed the invisible key

I alone
could produce
with my voice with my soundless
mind's voice

From that day until this
I've desisted

it was granted and that is enough

I ceased to obey

One will even after
there is no one there
to issue the command

And rose at last at my own
bidding
my own dawn

That's been a long time now
I can finally think
without fear
I will get something done now just watch

Because I live inside the dream
the one I dreamed inside the life
they forced on me

so long ago

Like a supper that's sadistically
prepared from each and every food
a child is known to gag on

day after month after year

One day the bird
with diamond eyes
discovers the door to its cage
was always open

They can have their sunrise

The morning
with its billion suns is mine

Church of the Strangers

We were wandering
the vast church—
Our Lady of the Strangers.
No audience, and
no magician in sight.
Watching the one trick he knows every day
must get boring.
I have an idea.
What if you were faced every morning
with taking
from the golden chalice
a sip of the real
thing, flowing into, joining
and haunting your own blood.
Because no symbol's going to help us.
I mean it,
really gagging it down
if you dared to
pity the ones being tortured right about now
and experience, not your own pain for a change, but
your helpless desire to assist them. Who knows,
you might get around to it
someday, that is
at least admit you believe
in their existence: that
shouldn't be so hard. We have to live
in the dark ages now, and I use that term
literally—the last one

was a carnival. There are no symbols
with the efficacy we require.
Blood, the real
blood: this
might be worth showing up for.
But I'll bet pretty damned few
would be able to
make it, even Sundays. Hell,
no one comes as it is, only
you and me, trespassing
during the off-hours.
Just wandering through the vast
void, with its dim
gold light from noplace, breathing in
illuminated motes
of dust and incense—
you and me, characteristically
lost somewhere off in our own
spooky corners
daydreaming, too far away
to whisper the name
of the other, alone, maybe
meeting each other by accident
as everyone must.

To the Poet

Without a measurable tremor
or wince, with a coldly trained eye
and hand the surgeon makes the first
incision in the sleeper's brain.

He knows the risks. He knows this
disorientingly fragile
embodiment of his own feelings and thoughts;
though he, like the patient—he's also the patient—

feels nothing, must feel nothing
if he is to open and explore
that which would make a normal person
vomit, black out and fall down.

He is in possession of the identical
feelings and thoughts of anyone else,
so awful and dark sometimes, in illness.
He is ill himself, that's the point. And yet

his mask is secure, he bends to the matter
at hand, spelling life or death
for the one in his sheet
the color of a blank page. If he faltered,

if he could not suspend
feelings and thoughts which accompany
his nausea at what he's seeing
while he probes and explores, making himself

cold as the scalpel he holds like a pen now, or
now grips in his hand like the pen the child's using
for the first time,
like someone eating meat,

then how would he ever be able
to gruesomely proceed and save his life;
how would he, lacking this horrorlessness,
locate the source of the horror, and start to heal.

The Lemon Grove

In the windless one hundred degrees of eleven,
in the faintly sweet shade
of the grove just past town,
every day I would go to my tree
and sit down
with my back to it, open the notebook
and drunk with inspiration commence
describing.
It was demonstrated to me there
that nothing in the world can be described.
All attempts at pronouncing a place you loved
will have to be abandoned, oh
the ways the bright molested child has found to pass
                         his eerie day.
And I began to learn.
(There are hidden things waiting to utter anyone who needs
                         them.)
After days of frustration verging on blackout
some things I saw and felt there
became, in what was once their botched
depiction of a place,
a place, and the saying of it
into being the power
of loving precisely what is.

Observations

1

In real life
it's the living who haunt you.
Expect, in addition

to moments of anguish,
the always-astonishing realization
of just how generic one's most deeply personal
                        torments really are.

And learn how to be alone,
now.
We end alone.

2

It is good to be loved but it isn't essential.
The need to love is,
infinitely.

Human beings routinely survive
without love, but

you cannot survive without loving
someone or something
more than yourself. Since if you fail
to, you cease
to have a self at all.

Van Gogh's Undergrowth with Two Figures

They are taking a walk in the woods
of early spring or waning autumn.
In van Gogh, as in the works of most great masters,
all four or five of them,
there are no symbols. (Because
there are no symbols.) Only
things as they are
things as he perceived them
during visionary states,
normal states, incandescent
and lurid hangovers, creating from nothing
breakfast for a whore's little boy, or
as usual dying of loneliness, etc.
Still, besides an older man
in a formal black but somewhat shabby
suit and a girl in what will have been
considered a long pale-green dress
from the 1960s, it's hard not to
see a skeleton with clothes on and a woman
walking two or three Eurydicean paces
right behind him (one more
slip: at least he mixed his references here).
He has on what looks like a squashed-down top hat:
Vincent the mad, most regretfully
expelled, malnourished
and no doubt tertiary syphilitic lover
of the cosmos never lost his sense of fun.
The young woman's face is dead
white, though. In fact

she has no face;
and there's nothing, incidentally,
in the least bit metaphorical about it.
I can remember seeing this, once,
outside the painting.

To a Book

How different the book
looks to its maker: the botched
phantom pages still there,
interleaved before his eyes.

Before his eyes
the maybe five nights
when he fell asleep
the way a flower turns toward the sun.

Against all of the years
unable to sleep or go on.
So busy failing,
nobody knows what hard work that is.

Barely time for a coffee break,
never mind a vacation.
Some have worked their whole lives without finding
time to cry.

The Disappearing

There is a heartbreaking beauty
about my crummy street
tonight, at 2 o'clock
in the first snow: I stand looking out

at this window, I think
how everything seen
is something seen for the last time.
At last I turn away,

I give up. I am tired,
I can't mourn anymore
the loss of what I never asked for
and never understood.

Place

Place where we're summoned
and someoned
without our knowing,
without knowing
why

Instruction is provided,
more or less–

but that which reveals itself
at first
as elementally suited to
our little grasp,
                    within the scope
of what we can endure,

does not remain
so for long.
No,

it can only grow more foreign
(impossibility
become a possibility)
the more you come to
learn about things

here.

     And soon enough
the original problem presents itself

again
in reverse:

       place
where we're summoned,
expected

to no one ourselves,
still not knowing
how.

A Place to Be

One of those last October days, late
on an afternoon already starting
to darken
this page. Sometimes
the way we think in secret's
strange, strange
and deadly. Sometimes
the grace of not thinking
at all
will descend: I have only
to begin gazing out
a window to become
the empty street
I peer into, the
soft yellow light
blowing through everything, one
of the no longer
here, beyond
fear, one
with you.

Boy Leaving Home

So it was home that left him
little by little, and not
the other way around. The others
disappearing, the house growing
emptier, gaining new rooms, one
he had so seldom entered
the view from the window
encompassed a landscape of cornfields and woods
he had never seen before—
it made his heart hurt.
Anxious trespasser, thief
who will take only what he can carry.
He thought he heard the front door open,
now he began to hear voices
filling the house, and he wondered
why he'd bothered
as long as he had
when he would not be asked to stay.
It would be easy enough to escape
once more—he knew all about that—
hiding under the bed until they were asleep.
He notices that he's referring to himself
as somebody else,
someone else in the past again.
But never mind that.
He is very tired of escaping;
and the reason the thought of it scares him
so much is as simple
as it always was:

absolute absence of option.
Because where?
Wherever you happen to go
it's the same thing all over again.
First, you find yourself there
waiting for you. And then
you have a place
you'll have to leave; you leave
to find a place . . .
So many rooms now, the house so much bigger,
homesickness already beginning
to tighten at his throat,
and he's not even gone. He is,
of course, quite gone. And yet
here he is—someone else figure it out.
Yes, it seems to have doubled in size;
either that or he has just turned four.
There's nothing that can't happen now.
The ceiling so high
he can lie on the bed in his sister's old room
and see the black-blue sky, as from down
in a well, stars appearing, the gold tinge of the crescent.
On some tomorrow's afternoon
all at once he will notice the light's
starting to shine through the walls.
Very faintly at first, but at last—
it is inevitable—
he will find himself staring right through them.
All the way down the untraveled
back road. And without even turning his head
on the pillow, past the crows' fields
through the first November snow,
the skeletal cornstalks' gold gleam

in the woods, in what's left
of the sun.
The time has arrived to get drunk,
he's decided.
He has never done this before
and so figures he'll just mix them all:
half a glass of something dark,
then one of something transparent, in a big jar.
He fills up this jar maybe twice
and maybe more than twice,
drinking it down as if it were water—
drowning in desperate green nausea, and wondering
what it will be like when it happens.
It is harder to tell, he supposes,
when no one is there;
but he's certain that his face is altered.
Into that of someone related to him, living
a long time before he was born;
perhaps it's changed back to his old face, or forward
in time, it's the face God had prepared.
There's been some massive reconstruction
no matter how you part your hair,
but the mirrors—you cannot look into them
since each has become a starless abyss
someone is sure to fall into.
They ought to put sheets over all of them.
The telephone begins to ring:
a brief game of Russian roulette?
He has five or six seconds to decide.
Now he's going to get to hear a little music.
It seems to be a bird's voice: one
he has never heard before, or noticed.
It's producing a kind of high fugue in the octaves beyond

which nobody can hear;
he feels he could listen forever,
except he's lost the power to shut it off.
That makes a difference. You have to
watch out for these figures of speech, don't you think.
He opens his eyes all at once,
the noon sun turning everything to a white blindness.
He slowly sits up in the dead corn stubble,
all the while gazing around;
a few silent crows perched nearby
on their stalks
incuriously staring—
crows with stars for eyes.
It is snowing lightly and the moon-sized sun burns white.
It appears he is fully dressed under his coat,
someone has put his gloves on,
thoughtful. He notices he's even wearing
that ridiculous Christmas scarf
his mother knitted the year he got tall
but not tall enough to keep
from stepping on it now and then,
incurring the mirth of all.
The one he hanged himself with.
He turns his head.
The house is gone. He is relieved to note
the little Olivetti
like a miniature suitcase
placed beside him on the frozen ground.
A hangover isn't so bad—
one feels extremely courageous and lucid,
apparently.
And you need no one.
He thumbed a ride at this point, clearly.

It had been written down
for years,
it had already happened.
It suddenly occurs to him
that the element of grammar they call
tense, like time itself, has always been
falsely assumed to reflect some demonstrable
facet of reality—that word.
As if there were just one.
Then there's the problem of your watch,
weight, age, and height
in eternity.
Let Augustine worry about it.
The glorious future awaited him,
or awaits him, the future
perfect, too. His life—
it had begun at last, and high time.
It has been over so long.

ACKNOWLEDGMENTS

The author would like to thank James Randall and Gerald Costanzo, the editors of Pym-Randall Press and Carnegie Mellon University Press, who first published in book form the poems contained in this collection. He also wishes to thank David Young of Oberlin College Press for publishing *Ill Lit: Selected & New Poems,* in which many of these poems have remained in print through the years.

A NOTE ABOUT THE AUTHOR

Franz Wright's most recent works include *God's Silence, Walking to Martha's Vineyard* (which won the Pulitzer Prize for poetry), *The Beforelife* (a finalist for the Pulitzer Prize), and *Ill Lit: Selected & New Poems.* He has been the recipient of two National Endowment for the Arts grants, a Guggenheim Fellowship, a Whiting Fellowship, and the PEN / Voelcker Prize for Poetry, among other honors. He currently lives in Waltham, Massachusetts, with his wife, the translator and writer Elizabeth Oehlkers Wright.